Music Practice Daily Record Notebook

This Notebook Belongs To

_____

Today

Date:_____

Main Goals

Subgoals

Start Time:_____ Stop:_____ Total Time:_____

Warm-ups	Scales
1	1
2	2
3	3
4	4

Repertoire & Exercises

Notes & Focus

Additional Tasks

- ◯
- ◯
- ◯
- ◯

Music Listening

- ◯
- ◯
- ◯

Today

Date:_____

Main Goals

Subgoals

Start Time:_____ Stop:_____ Total Time:_____

Warm-ups		Scales	
1		1	
2		2	
3		3	
4		4	

Repertoire & Exercises

Notes & Focus

Additional Tasks

- ◯
- ◯
- ◯
- ◯

Music Listening

- ◯
- ◯
- ◯

Today

Date:_____

Main Goals

Subgoals

Start Time:_____ Stop:_____ Total Time: _____

Warm-ups

1
2
3
4

Scales

1
2
3
4

Repertoire & Exercises

Notes & Focus

Additional Tasks

○
○
○
○

Music Listening

○
○
○

Today

Date:_____

Main Goals

Subgoals

Start Time:_____ Stop:_____ Total Time: _____

Warm-ups	Scales
1	1
2	2
3	3
4	4

Repertoire & Exercises

Notes & Focus

Additional Tasks

○
○
○
○

Music Listening

○
○
○

Today

Date:_____

Main Goals

Subgoals

Start Time:_____ Stop:_____ Total Time: _____

Warm-ups		Scales	
1		1	
2		2	
3		3	
4		4	

Repertoire & Exercises

Notes & Focus

Additional Tasks

○
○
○
○

Music Listening

○
○
○

Today

Date:_____

Main Goals

Subgoals

Start Time:_____ Stop:_____ Total Time: _____

Warm-ups	Scales
1	1
2	2
3	3
4	4

Repertoire & Exercises

Notes & Focus

Additional Tasks

- ◯
- ◯
- ◯
- ◯

Music Listening

- ◯
- ◯
- ◯

Today

Date:_____

Main Goals

Subgoals

Start Time:_____ Stop:_____ Total Time: _____

Warm-ups		Scales	
1		1	
2		2	
3		3	
4		4	

Repertoire & Exercises

Notes & Focus

Additional Tasks

○
○
○
○

Music Listening

○
○
○

Today

Date:_____

Main Goals

Subgoals

Start Time:_____ Stop:_____ Total Time: _____

Warm-ups		Scales	
1		1	
2		2	
3		3	
4		4	

Repertoire & Exercises

Notes & Focus

Additional Tasks

○
○
○
○

Music Listening

○
○
○

Today

Date:_____

Main Goals

Subgoals

Start Time:_____ Stop:_____ Total Time: _____

Warm-ups		Scales	
1		1	
2		2	
3		3	
4		4	

Repertoire & Exercises

Notes & Focus

Additional Tasks

○

○

○

○

Music Listening

○

○

○

Today

Date:_____

Main Goals

Subgoals

Start Time:_____ Stop:_____ Total Time:_____

Warm-ups	
1	
2	
3	
4	

Scales	
1	
2	
3	
4	

Repertoire & Exercises

Notes & Focus

Additional Tasks

○

○

○

○

Music Listening

○

○

○

Today

Date:_____

Main Goals

Subgoals

Start Time:_____ Stop:_____ Total Time: _____

Warm-ups		Scales	
1		1	
2		2	
3		3	
4		4	

Repertoire & Exercises

Notes & Focus

Additional Tasks

○

○

○

○

Music Listening

○

○

○

Today

Date:_____

Main Goals

Subgoals

Start Time:_____ Stop:_____ Total Time: _____

Warm-ups		Scales	
1		1	
2		2	
3		3	
4		4	

Repertoire & Exercises

Notes & Focus

Additional Tasks

- ◯
- ◯
- ◯
- ◯

Music Listening

- ◯
- ◯
- ◯

Today

Date:_____

Main Goals

Subgoals

Start Time:_____ Stop:_____ Total Time: _____

Warm-ups		Scales	
1		1	
2		2	
3		3	
4		4	

Repertoire & Exercises

Notes & Focus

Additional Tasks

○
○
○
○

Music Listening

○
○
○

Today

Date:_____

Main Goals

Subgoals

Start Time:_____ Stop:_____ Total Time: _____

Warm-ups		Scales	
1		1	
2		2	
3		3	
4		4	

Repertoire & Exercises

Notes & Focus

Additional Tasks

○
○
○
○

Music Listening

○
○
○

Today

Date:_____

Main Goals

Subgoals

Start Time:_____ Stop:_____ Total Time:_____

Warm-ups		Scales	
1		1	
2		2	
3		3	
4		4	

Repertoire & Exercises

Notes & Focus

Additional Tasks

- ◯
- ◯
- ◯
- ◯

Music Listening

- ◯
- ◯
- ◯

Today

Date:_____

Main Goals

Subgoals

Start Time:_____ Stop:_____ Total Time: _____

Warm-ups	Scales
1	1
2	2
3	3
4	4

Repertoire & Exercises

Notes & Focus

Additional Tasks

○
○
○
○

Music Listening

○
○
○

Today

Date:_____

Main Goals

Subgoals

Start Time:_____   Stop:_____   Total Time:_____

Warm-ups	Scales
1	1
2	2
3	3
4	4

Repertoire & Exercises

Notes & Focus

Additional Tasks

- ◯
- ◯
- ◯
- ◯

Music Listening

- ◯
- ◯
- ◯

Today

Date:_____

Main Goals

Subgoals

Start Time:_____ Stop:_____ Total Time:_____

Warm-ups	Scales
1	1
2	2
3	3
4	4

Repertoire & Exercises

Notes & Focus

Additional Tasks

- ◯
- ◯
- ◯
- ◯

Music Listening

- ◯
- ◯
- ◯

Today

Date:_____

Main Goals

Subgoals

Start Time:_____ Stop:_____ Total Time: _____

Warm-ups	Scales
1	1
2	2
3	3
4	4

Repertoire & Exercises

Notes & Focus

Additional Tasks

○
○
○
○

Music Listening

○
○
○

Today

Date:_____

Main Goals

Subgoals

Start Time:_____ Stop:_____ Total Time: _____

Warm-ups		Scales	
1		1	
2		2	
3		3	
4		4	

Repertoire & Exercises

Notes & Focus

Additional Tasks

◯
◯
◯
◯

Music Listening

◯
◯
◯

Today

Date:_____

Main Goals

Subgoals

Start Time:_____ Stop:_____ Total Time: _____

Warm-ups		Scales	
1		1	
2		2	
3		3	
4		4	

Repertoire & Exercises

Notes & Focus

Additional Tasks

- ○
- ○
- ○
- ○

Music Listening

- ○
- ○
- ○

Today

Date:_____

Main Goals

Subgoals

Start Time:_____ Stop:_____ Total Time: _____

Warm-ups		Scales	
1		1	
2		2	
3		3	
4		4	

Repertoire & Exercises

Notes & Focus

Additional Tasks

○
○
○
○

Music Listening

○
○
○

Today

Date:_____

Main Goals

Subgoals

Start Time:_____ Stop:_____ Total Time: _____

Warm-ups	Scales
1	1
2	2
3	3
4	4

Repertoire & Exercises

Notes & Focus

Additional Tasks

- ◯
- ◯
- ◯
- ◯

Music Listening

- ◯
- ◯
- ◯

Today

Date:_____

Main Goals

Subgoals

Start Time:_____ Stop:_____ Total Time: _____

Warm-ups		Scales	
1		1	
2		2	
3		3	
4		4	

Repertoire & Exercises

Notes & Focus

Additional Tasks

◯
◯
◯
◯

Music Listening

◯
◯
◯

Today

Date:_____

Main Goals

Subgoals

Start Time:_____ Stop:_____ Total Time: _____

Warm-ups	Scales
1	1
2	2
3	3
4	4

Repertoire & Exercises

Notes & Focus

Additional Tasks

○
○
○
○

Music Listening

○
○
○

Today

Date:_____

Main Goals

Subgoals

Start Time:_____ Stop:_____ Total Time: _____

Warm-ups		Scales	
1		1	
2		2	
3		3	
4		4	

Repertoire & Exercises

Notes & Focus

Additional Tasks

○

○

○

○

Music Listening

○

○

○

Today

Date:_____

Main Goals

Subgoals

Start Time:_____ Stop:_____ Total Time:_____

Warm-ups		Scales	
1		1	
2		2	
3		3	
4		4	

Repertoire & Exercises

Notes & Focus

Additional Tasks

- ◯
- ◯
- ◯
- ◯

Music Listening

- ◯
- ◯
- ◯

Today

Date:_____

Main Goals

Subgoals

Start Time:_____ Stop:_____ Total Time: _____

Warm-ups	Scales
1	1
2	2
3	3
4	4

Repertoire & Exercises

Notes & Focus

Additional Tasks

○
○
○
○

Music Listening

○
○
○

Today

Date:_____

Main Goals

Subgoals

Start Time:_____   Stop:_____   Total Time: _____

Warm-ups		Scales	
1		1	
2		2	
3		3	
4		4	

Repertoire & Exercises

Notes & Focus

Additional Tasks

- ◯
- ◯
- ◯
- ◯

Music Listening

- ◯
- ◯
- ◯

Today

Date:_____

Main Goals

Subgoals

Start Time:_____ Stop:_____ Total Time: _____

Warm-ups		Scales	
1		1	
2		2	
3		3	
4		4	

Repertoire & Exercises

Notes & Focus

Additional Tasks

○
○
○
○

Music Listening

○
○
○

Today

Date:_____

Main Goals

Subgoals

Start Time:_____ Stop:_____ Total Time: _____

Warm-ups

1
2
3
4

Scales

1
2
3
4

Repertoire & Exercises

Notes & Focus

Additional Tasks

- ◯
- ◯
- ◯
- ◯

Music Listening

- ◯
- ◯
- ◯

Today

Date:_____

Main Goals

Subgoals

Start Time:_____ Stop:_____ Total Time: _____

Warm-ups		Scales	
1		1	
2		2	
3		3	
4		4	

Repertoire & Exercises

Notes & Focus

Additional Tasks

◯
◯
◯
◯

Music Listening

◯
◯
◯

Today

Date:_____

Main Goals

Subgoals

Start Time:_____   Stop:_____   Total Time: _____

Warm-ups	Scales
1	1
2	2
3	3
4	4

Repertoire & Exercises

Notes & Focus

Additional Tasks

- ◯
- ◯
- ◯
- ◯

Music Listening

- ◯
- ◯
- ◯

Today

Date:_____

Main Goals

Subgoals

Start Time:_____ Stop:_____ Total Time: _____

Warm-ups		Scales	
1		1	
2		2	
3		3	
4		4	

Repertoire & Exercises

Notes & Focus

Additional Tasks

○
○
○
○

Music Listening

○
○
○

Today

Date:_____

Main Goals

Subgoals

Start Time:_____ Stop:_____ Total Time:_____

Warm-ups

1	
2	
3	
4	

Scales

1	
2	
3	
4	

Repertoire & Exercises

Notes & Focus

Additional Tasks

- ◯
- ◯
- ◯
- ◯

Music Listening

- ◯
- ◯
- ◯

Today

Date:_____

Main Goals

Subgoals

Start Time:_____ Stop:_____ Total Time: _____

Warm-ups		Scales	
1		1	
2		2	
3		3	
4		4	

Repertoire & Exercises

Notes & Focus

Additional Tasks

- ○
- ○
- ○
- ○

Music Listening

- ○
- ○
- ○
- ○

Today

Date:_____

Main Goals

Subgoals

Start Time:_____ Stop:_____ Total Time:_____

Warm-ups	Scales
1	1
2	2
3	3
4	4

Repertoire & Exercises

Notes & Focus

Additional Tasks
- ○
- ○
- ○
- ○

Music Listening
- ○
- ○
- ○

Today

Date:_____

Main Goals

Subgoals

Start Time:_____ Stop:_____ Total Time: _____

Warm-ups	Scales
1	1
2	2
3	3
4	4

Repertoire & Exercises

Notes & Focus

Additional Tasks

○
○
○
○

Music Listening

○
○
○

Today

Date:_____

Main Goals

Subgoals

Start Time:_____ Stop:_____ Total Time:_____

Warm-ups

1
2
3
4

Scales

1
2
3
4

Repertoire & Exercises

Notes & Focus

Additional Tasks

○
○
○
○

Music Listening

○
○
○

Today

Date:_____

Main Goals

Subgoals

Start Time:_____ Stop:_____ Total Time: _____

Warm-ups		Scales	
1		1	
2		2	
3		3	
4		4	

Repertoire & Exercises

Notes & Focus

Additional Tasks

- ◯
- ◯
- ◯
- ◯

Music Listening

- ◯
- ◯
- ◯

Today

Date:_____

Main Goals

Subgoals

Start Time:_____ Stop:_____ Total Time: _____

Warm-ups

1

2

3

4

Scales

1

2

3

4

Repertoire & Exercises

Notes & Focus

Additional Tasks

◯

◯

◯

◯

Music Listening

◯

◯

◯

Today

Date:_____

Main Goals

Subgoals

Start Time:_____   Stop:_____   Total Time: _____

Warm-ups		Scales	
1		1	
2		2	
3		3	
4		4	

Repertoire & Exercises

Notes & Focus

Additional Tasks

○
○
○
○

Music Listening

○
○
○

Today

Date:_____

Main Goals

Subgoals

Start Time:_____ Stop:_____ Total Time: _____

Warm-ups

1

2

3

4

Scales

1

2

3

4

Repertoire & Exercises

Notes & Focus

Additional Tasks

- ◯
- ◯
- ◯
- ◯

Music Listening

- ◯
- ◯
- ◯

Today

Date:_____

Main Goals

Subgoals

Start Time:_____ Stop:_____ Total Time: _____

Warm-ups	Scales
1	1
2	2
3	3
4	4

Repertoire & Exercises

Notes & Focus

Additional Tasks

◯
◯
◯
◯

Music Listening

◯
◯
◯

Today

Date:_____

Main Goals

Subgoals

Start Time:_____ Stop:_____ Total Time:_____

Warm-ups

1
2
3
4

Scales

1
2
3
4

Repertoire & Exercises

Notes & Focus

Additional Tasks

○
○
○
○

Music Listening

○
○
○

Today

Date:_____

Main Goals

Subgoals

Start Time:_____ Stop:_____ Total Time:_____

Warm-ups		Scales	
1		1	
2		2	
3		3	
4		4	

Repertoire & Exercises

Notes & Focus

Additional Tasks

- ◯
- ◯
- ◯
- ◯

Music Listening

- ◯
- ◯
- ◯

Today

Date:_____

Main Goals

Subgoals

Start Time:_____ Stop:_____ Total Time: _____

Warm-ups		Scales	
1		1	
2		2	
3		3	
4		4	

Repertoire & Exercises

Notes & Focus

Additional Tasks

- ◯
- ◯
- ◯
- ◯

Music Listening

- ◯
- ◯
- ◯

Today

Date:_____

Main Goals

Subgoals

Start Time:_____ Stop:_____ Total Time: _____

Warm-ups		Scales	
1		1	
2		2	
3		3	
4		4	

Repertoire & Exercises

Notes & Focus

Additional Tasks
- ◯
- ◯
- ◯
- ◯

Music Listening
- ◯
- ◯
- ◯

Today

Date:_____

Main Goals

Subgoals

Start Time:_____   Stop:_____   Total Time: _____

Warm-ups		Scales	
1		1	
2		2	
3		3	
4		4	

Repertoire & Exercises

Notes & Focus

Additional Tasks

- ◯
- ◯
- ◯
- ◯

Music Listening

- ◯
- ◯
- ◯

Today

Date:_____

Main Goals

Subgoals

Start Time:_____ Stop:_____ Total Time: _____

Warm-ups	Scales
1	1
2	2
3	3
4	4

Repertoire & Exercises

Notes & Focus

Additional Tasks

○
○
○
○

Music Listening

○
○
○

Today

Date:_____

Main Goals

Subgoals

Start Time:_____ Stop:_____   Total Time: _____

Warm-ups	Scales
1	1
2	2
3	3
4	4

Repertoire & Exercises

Notes & Focus

Additional Tasks

- ◯
- ◯
- ◯
- ◯

Music Listening

- ◯
- ◯
- ◯

Today

Date:_____

Main Goals

Subgoals

Start Time:_____ Stop:_____ Total Time:_____

Warm-ups		Scales	
1		1	
2		2	
3		3	
4		4	

Repertoire & Exercises

Notes & Focus

Additional Tasks

- ◯
- ◯
- ◯
- ◯

Music Listening

- ◯
- ◯
- ◯

Today

Date:_____

Main Goals

Subgoals

Start Time:_____ Stop:_____ Total Time: _____

Warm-ups		Scales	
1		1	
2		2	
3		3	
4		4	

Repertoire & Exercises

Notes & Focus

Additional Tasks

○
○
○
○

Music Listening

○
○
○

Today

Date:_____

Main Goals

Subgoals

Start Time:_____ Stop:_____ Total Time: _____

Warm-ups	Scales
1	1
2	2
3	3
4	4

Repertoire & Exercises

Notes & Focus

Additional Tasks

○
○
○
○

Music Listening

○
○
○

Today

Date:_____

Main Goals

Subgoals

Start Time:_____ Stop:_____ Total Time: _____

Warm-ups	Scales
1	1
2	2
3	3
4	4

Repertoire & Exercises

Notes & Focus

Additional Tasks

◯
◯
◯
◯

Music Listening

◯
◯
◯

Today

Date:_____

Main Goals

Subgoals

Start Time:_____ Stop:_____ Total Time:_____

Warm-ups		Scales	
1		1	
2		2	
3		3	
4		4	

Repertoire & Exercises

Notes & Focus

Additional Tasks

- ◯
- ◯
- ◯
- ◯

Music Listening

- ◯
- ◯
- ◯

Today

Date:_____

Main Goals

Subgoals

Start Time:_____   Stop:_____   Total Time: _____

Warm-ups
1
2
3
4

Scales
1
2
3
4

Repertoire & Exercises

Notes & Focus

Additional Tasks
- ◯
- ◯
- ◯
- ◯

Music Listening
- ◯
- ◯
- ◯

Today

Date:_____

Main Goals

Subgoals

Start Time:_____ Stop:_____ Total Time: _____

Warm-ups	Scales
1	1
2	2
3	3
4	4

Repertoire & Exercises

Notes & Focus

Additional Tasks

○
○
○
○

Music Listening

○
○
○

Today

Date:_____

Main Goals

Subgoals

Start Time:_____ Stop:_____ Total Time:_____

Warm-ups	Scales
1	1
2	2
3	3
4	4

Repertoire & Exercises

Notes & Focus

Additional Tasks

- ○
- ○
- ○
- ○

Music Listening

- ○
- ○
- ○

Today

Date:_____

Main Goals

Subgoals

Start Time:_____ Stop:_____ Total Time: _____

Warm-ups	Scales
1	1
2	2
3	3
4	4

Repertoire & Exercises

Notes & Focus

Additional Tasks

- ◯
- ◯
- ◯
- ◯

Music Listening

- ◯
- ◯
- ◯

Today

Date:_____

Main Goals

Subgoals

Start Time:_____ Stop:_____ Total Time:_____

Warm-ups	Scales
1	1
2	2
3	3
4	4

Repertoire & Exercises

Notes & Focus

Additional Tasks

- ◯
- ◯
- ◯
- ◯

Music Listening

- ◯
- ◯
- ◯

Today

Date:_____

Main Goals

Subgoals

Start Time:_____ Stop:_____ Total Time: _____

Warm-ups		Scales	
1		1	
2		2	
3		3	
4		4	

Repertoire & Exercises

Notes & Focus

Additional Tasks

○
○
○
○

Music Listening

○
○
○

Today

Date:_____

Main Goals

Subgoals

Start Time:_____ Stop:_____ Total Time: _____

Warm-ups

1
2
3
4

Scales

1
2
3
4

Repertoire & Exercises

Notes & Focus

Additional Tasks

○
○
○
○

Music Listening

○
○
○

Today

Date:_____

Main Goals

Subgoals

Start Time:_____ Stop:_____ Total Time:_____

Warm-ups		Scales	
1		1	
2		2	
3		3	
4		4	

Repertoire & Exercises

Notes & Focus

Additional Tasks

○
○
○
○

Music Listening

○
○
○

Today

Date:_____

Main Goals

Subgoals

Start Time:_____ Stop:_____ Total Time: _____

Warm-ups	Scales
1	1
2	2
3	3
4	4

Repertoire & Exercises

Notes & Focus

Additional Tasks

- ◯
- ◯
- ◯
- ◯

Music Listening

- ◯
- ◯
- ◯

Today

Date:_____

Main Goals

Subgoals

Start Time:_____   Stop:_____   Total Time:_____

Warm-ups		Scales	
1		1	
2		2	
3		3	
4		4	

Repertoire & Exercises

Notes & Focus

Additional Tasks

- ◯
- ◯
- ◯
- ◯

Music Listening

- ◯
- ◯
- ◯

Today

Date:_____

Main Goals

Subgoals

Start Time:_____ Stop:_____ Total Time:_____

Warm-ups		Scales	
1		1	
2		2	
3		3	
4		4	

Repertoire & Exercises

Notes & Focus

Additional Tasks

- ◯
- ◯
- ◯
- ◯

Music Listening

- ◯
- ◯
- ◯

Today

Date:_____

Main Goals

Subgoals

Start Time:_____ Stop:_____ Total Time: _____

Warm-ups		Scales	
1		1	
2		2	
3		3	
4		4	

Repertoire & Exercises

Notes & Focus

Additional Tasks

- ◯
- ◯
- ◯
- ◯

Music Listening

- ◯
- ◯
- ◯

Today

Date:_____

Main Goals

Subgoals

Start Time:_____ Stop:_____ Total Time: _____

Warm-ups		Scales	
1		1	
2		2	
3		3	
4		4	

Repertoire & Exercises

Notes & Focus

Additional Tasks

- ◯
- ◯
- ◯
- ◯

Music Listening

- ◯
- ◯
- ◯

Today

Date:_____

Main Goals

Subgoals

Start Time:_____ Stop:_____ Total Time:_____

Warm-ups		Scales	
1		1	
2		2	
3		3	
4		4	

Repertoire & Exercises

Notes & Focus

Additional Tasks

- ○
- ○
- ○
- ○

Music Listening

- ○
- ○
- ○

Today

Date:_____

Main Goals

Subgoals

Start Time:_____ Stop:_____ Total Time:_____

Warm-ups	Scales
1	1
2	2
3	3
4	4

Repertoire & Exercises

Notes & Focus

Additional Tasks

- ◯
- ◯
- ◯
- ◯

Music Listening

- ◯
- ◯
- ◯

Today

Date:_____

Main Goals

Subgoals

Start Time:_____ Stop:_____ Total Time: _____

Warm-ups

1	
2	
3	
4	

Scales

1	
2	
3	
4	

Repertoire & Exercises

Notes & Focus

Additional Tasks

○
○
○
○

Music Listening

○
○
○

Today

Date:_____

Main Goals

Subgoals

Start Time:_____ Stop:_____ Total Time: _____

Warm-ups		Scales	
1		1	
2		2	
3		3	
4		4	

Repertoire & Exercises

Notes & Focus

Additional Tasks

○

○

○

○

Music Listening

○

○

○

Today

Date:_____

Main Goals

Subgoals

Start Time:_____ Stop:_____ Total Time: _____

Warm-ups	Scales
1	1
2	2
3	3
4	4

Repertoire & Exercises

Notes & Focus

Additional Tasks

○
○
○
○

Music Listening

○
○
○

Today

Date:_____

Main Goals

Subgoals

Start Time:_____ Stop:_____ Total Time: _____

Warm-ups	Scales
1	1
2	2
3	3
4	4

Repertoire & Exercises

Notes & Focus

Additional Tasks

- ◯
- ◯
- ◯
- ◯

Music Listening

- ◯
- ◯
- ◯

Today

Date:_____

Main Goals

Subgoals

Start Time:_____ Stop:_____ Total Time: _____

Warm-ups	Scales
1	1
2	2
3	3
4	4

Repertoire & Exercises

Notes & Focus

Additional Tasks

○

○

○

○

Music Listening

○

○

○

Today

Date:_____

Main Goals

Subgoals

Start Time:_____ Stop:_____ Total Time:_____

Warm-ups

1
2
3
4

Scales

1
2
3
4

Repertoire & Exercises

Notes & Focus

Additional Tasks

- ○
- ○
- ○
- ○

Music Listening

- ○
- ○
- ○

Today

Date:_____

Main Goals

Subgoals

Start Time:_____ Stop:_____ Total Time: _____

Warm-ups	Scales
1	1
2	2
3	3
4	4

Repertoire & Exercises

Notes & Focus

Additional Tasks

◯
◯
◯
◯

Music Listening

◯
◯
◯

Today

Date:_____

Main Goals

Subgoals

Start Time:_____ Stop:_____ Total Time: _____

Warm-ups	Scales
1	1
2	2
3	3
4	4

Repertoire & Exercises

Notes & Focus

Additional Tasks

- ◯
- ◯
- ◯
- ◯

Music Listening

- ◯
- ◯
- ◯

Today

Date:_____

Main Goals

Subgoals

Start Time:_____ Stop:_____ Total Time:_____

Warm-ups	Scales
1	1
2	2
3	3
4	4

Repertoire & Exercises

Notes & Focus

Additional Tasks

◯

◯

◯

◯

Music Listening

◯

◯

◯

Today

Date:_____

Main Goals

Subgoals

Start Time:_____ Stop:_____ Total Time:_____

Warm-ups

1	
2	
3	
4	

Scales

1	
2	
3	
4	

Repertoire & Exercises

Notes & Focus

Additional Tasks

- ◯
- ◯
- ◯
- ◯

Music Listening

- ◯
- ◯
- ◯

Today

Date:_____

Main Goals

Subgoals

Start Time:_____ Stop:_____ Total Time: _____

Warm-ups		Scales	
1		1	
2		2	
3		3	
4		4	

Repertoire & Exercises

Notes & Focus

Additional Tasks

- ◯
- ◯
- ◯
- ◯

Music Listening

- ◯
- ◯
- ◯

Today

Date:_____

Main Goals

Subgoals

Start Time:_____ Stop:_____ Total Time: _____

Warm-ups	Scales
1	1
2	2
3	3
4	4

Repertoire & Exercises

Notes & Focus

Additional Tasks

○
○
○
○

Music Listening

○
○
○

Today

Date:_____

Main Goals

Subgoals

Start Time:_____   Stop:_____   Total Time: _____

Warm-ups	Scales
1	1
2	2
3	3
4	4

Repertoire & Exercises

Notes & Focus

Additional Tasks

○
○
○
○

Music Listening

○
○
○

Today

Date:_____

Main Goals	Subgoals

Start Time:_____ Stop:_____ Total Time: _____

Warm-ups	Scales
1	1
2	2
3	3
4	4

Repertoire & Exercises

Notes & Focus

Additional Tasks

- ◯
- ◯
- ◯
- ◯

Music Listening

- ◯
- ◯
- ◯

Today

Date:_____

Main Goals

Subgoals

Start Time:_____   Stop:_____   Total Time:_____

Warm-ups		Scales	
1		1	
2		2	
3		3	
4		4	

Repertoire & Exercises

Notes & Focus

Additional Tasks

◯
◯
◯
◯

Music Listening

◯
◯
◯

Today

Date:_____

Main Goals	Subgoals

Start Time:_____ Stop:_____ Total Time: _____

Warm-ups	Scales
1	1
2	2
3	3
4	4

Repertoire & Exercises

Notes & Focus

Additional Tasks

○
○
○
○

Music Listening

○
○
○

Today

Date:_____

Main Goals

Subgoals

Start Time:_____ Stop:_____ Total Time: _____

Warm-ups		Scales	
1		1	
2		2	
3		3	
4		4	

Repertoire & Exercises

Notes & Focus

Additional Tasks

○
○
○
○

Music Listening

○
○
○

Today

Date:_____

Main Goals

Subgoals

Start Time:_____ Stop:_____ Total Time:_____

Warm-ups	Scales
1	1
2	2
3	3
4	4

Repertoire & Exercises

Notes & Focus

Additional Tasks

- ◯
- ◯
- ◯
- ◯

Music Listening

- ◯
- ◯
- ◯

Today

Date:_____

Main Goals

Subgoals

Start Time:_____ Stop:_____ Total Time:_____

Warm-ups	Scales
1	1
2	2
3	3
4	4

Repertoire & Exercises

Notes & Focus

Additional Tasks

○
○
○
○

Music Listening

○
○
○

Today

Date:_____

Main Goals

Subgoals

Start Time:_____ Stop:_____ Total Time: _____

Warm-ups		Scales	
1		1	
2		2	
3		3	
4		4	

Repertoire & Exercises

Notes & Focus

Additional Tasks

○
○
○
○

Music Listening

○
○
○

Today

Date:_____

Main Goals

Subgoals

Start Time:_____ Stop:_____ Total Time: _____

Warm-ups		Scales	
1		1	
2		2	
3		3	
4		4	

Repertoire & Exercises

Notes & Focus

Additional Tasks

- ◯
- ◯
- ◯
- ◯

Music Listening

- ◯
- ◯
- ◯

Today

Date:_____

Main Goals

Subgoals

Start Time:_____ Stop:_____ Total Time:_____

Warm-ups		Scales	
1		1	
2		2	
3		3	
4		4	

Repertoire & Exercises

Notes & Focus

Additional Tasks

◯

◯

◯

◯

Music Listening

◯

◯

◯

Today

Date:_____

Main Goals

Subgoals

Start Time:_____ Stop:_____ Total Time: _____

Warm-ups		Scales	
1		1	
2		2	
3		3	
4		4	

Repertoire & Exercises

Notes & Focus

Additional Tasks

- ◯
- ◯
- ◯
- ◯

Music Listening

- ◯
- ◯
- ◯

Today

Date:_____

Main Goals

Subgoals

Start Time:_____ Stop:_____ Total Time:_____

Warm-ups	Scales
1	1
2	2
3	3
4	4

Repertoire & Exercises

Notes & Focus

Additional Tasks

- ○
- ○
- ○
- ○

Music Listening

- ○
- ○
- ○

Today

Date:_____

Main Goals

Subgoals

Start Time:_____ Stop:_____ Total Time: _____

Warm-ups	Scales
1	1
2	2
3	3
4	4

Repertoire & Exercises

Notes & Focus

Additional Tasks

- ◯
- ◯
- ◯
- ◯

Music Listening

- ◯
- ◯
- ◯
- ◯

Today

Date:_____

Main Goals

Subgoals

Start Time:_____ Stop:_____ Total Time:_____

Warm-ups

1
2
3
4

Scales

1
2
3
4

Repertoire & Exercises

Notes & Focus

Additional Tasks

○
○
○
○

Music Listening

○
○
○

Today

Date:_____

Main Goals

Subgoals

Start Time:_____ Stop:_____ Total Time:_____

Warm-ups		Scales	
1		1	
2		2	
3		3	
4		4	

Repertoire & Exercises

Notes & Focus

Additional Tasks

- ○
- ○
- ○
- ○

Music Listening

- ○
- ○
- ○

Today

Date:_____

Main Goals

Subgoals

Start Time:_____ Stop:_____ Total Time: _____

Warm-ups		Scales	
1		1	
2		2	
3		3	
4		4	

Repertoire & Exercises

Notes & Focus

Additional Tasks

○

○

○

○

Music Listening

○

○

○

Today

Date:_____

Main Goals

Subgoals

Start Time:_____ Stop:_____ Total Time:_____

Warm-ups	Scales
1	1
2	2
3	3
4	4

Repertoire & Exercises

Notes & Focus

Additional Tasks

- ◯
- ◯
- ◯
- ◯

Music Listening

- ◯
- ◯
- ◯